The Wizard of Oz

LEVEL 3

Original story by: L. Frank Baum
Re-told by: Helen Parker
Series Editor: Melanie Williams

Pearson Education Limited
Edinburgh Gate, Harlow,
Essex CM20 2JE, England
and Associated Companies throughout the world.

ISBN: 978-1-4082-8834-4

This edition first published by Pearson Education Ltd 2014

7 9 10 8

Set in 17/21pt OT Fiendstar
Printed in China
SWTC/07

Illustrations: Nikolas Ilic

Published by Pearson Education Ltd.

*Every effort has been made to trace the copyright holders and we apologise in advance for any unintentional omissions.
We would be pleased to insert the appropriate acknowledgement in any subsequent edition of this publication.*

For a complete list of the titles available in the Pearson English Kids Readers series, please go to
www.pearsonenglishkidsreaders.com. Alternatively, write to your local Pearson Education office or to
Pearson English Readers Marketing Department, Pearson Education, Edinburgh Gate, Harlow, Essex CM202JE, England.

Dorothy lives on a farm with her Aunt Em
and her Uncle Henry.

One day, the sky goes
very dark. "Oh, no!
A storm is coming!"
Dorothy says.

She runs to the house
with her dog, Toto.

It is very windy! Suddenly, the house flies up into the sky. The house goes around and around and around in the strong wind.

around and around and around

Dorothy is very scared. "Let's hide under the bed!" she says to Toto.

Then the house falls
down and down ...

cRASH!

The house falls on the Bad Witch of the East! It kills the
witch. Dorothy sees the witch's legs under the house.
The witch has very beautiful shoes on her feet.

"Welcome to Oz," a beautiful woman says. "I'm the Good Witch of the North."

"I want to go home!" Dorothy cries.

"Take these shoes and find the Wizard of Oz," the good witch says. "Then you can go home."

"But how can I find the Wizard?" Dorothy asks.

"Follow the yellow brick road!" the Good Witch of the North answers. "The Wizard lives in the City of Oz."

Dorothy takes Toto in her arms and walks down the road.

"Hello!" the Scarecrow shouts.
"What are you doing?"

"I'm looking for the Wizard of Oz,"
Dorothy answers.

"I want to be smart,"
the Scarecrow says. "Can
the Wizard give me a brain?"

"Yes! Come with me,"
Dorothy answers.

Dorothy and the Scarecrow go through a forest.
They see a man between the trees – the Tin Man.

"Are you okay?" Dorothy asks.

"No," the man says. "I can't move!"

Dorothy puts oil on the Tin Man's
arms and legs.

"I can move!" the Tin Man says. "What are you doing?"

"We're looking for the Wizard of Oz."

"Can the Wizard give me a heart?" the Tin Man asks.
"I want to have feelings."

"Yes!" Dorothy says. "Come with us!"

Dorothy and her friends walk down the yellow brick road. Suddenly, the Lion jumps out of the forest and roars at Toto.

"Don't hurt Toto!" Dorothy cries. "He's only small!"

"I'm very sorry," the Lion says. "I'm a big coward!"

The Lion is very sad. Now he is crying.

Dorothy wants to help the Lion. "Come with us," she says. "The Wizard of Oz can give you courage."

"Thank you," the Lion answers. "I want to be brave!"

Dorothy, Toto, the Scarecrow, the Tin Man,
and the Lion walk down the yellow brick road.
They walk for a long time.

At last they see a big green city – the City of Oz.
Dorothy asks for the Wizard.

Dorothy goes into a dark room. She sees a big head —
it is the Wizard of Oz!

"I want to go home," Dorothy says.

"Kill the Bad Witch of the West," the Wizard tells her.
"Then you can go home!"

The witch puts Dorothy's friends into a room and closes the door. They cannot leave!

"You have to work for me now!" the witch tells Dorothy.

Dorothy has to wash the floors. The witch sees Dorothy's shoes and wants them. The witch puts her hand on a shoe ...

Dorothy throws water at the witch! The witch gets

smaller

and

smaller!

HOORAY!
The witch is dead!

Dorothy and her friends are happy!
They go to Oz. They look for the
Wizard. But where is he?

Who is this small man?

"I'm the Wizard," the small
man says. "I arrived here many
years ago in my balloon."

"I wanted to help Oz," the Wizard says. "Now the bad witches are dead, I can go home! Thank you!"

The Wizard gives a brain to the Scarecrow, a heart to the Tin Man and courage to the Lion.

"I'm leaving now," the Wizard says.
"Dorothy, I can take you home."

Dorothy says goodbye to her
friends. She gets into the balloon.
But Toto jumps from her arms ...

Dorothy jumps out of the
balloon. She has to find Toto.

Dorothy finds Toto. But how can she go home now?

"Go and see the Good Witch of the South," a man says. "She can help you."

Dorothy and her friends go to the good witch's castle.

"Click your shoes three times,"
the Good Witch of the South says.
"Then you can go home!"

Dorothy clicks her shoes
ONE ... TWO ... THREE times.

"Goodbye, my friends!" she shouts.

WHOOSH! Dorothy goes ...

around and around

... and arrives back at the farm with Toto.

Aunt Em and Uncle Henry run to Dorothy and hold her in their arms.

Dorothy is very happy. At last she is at home with her family.

Activity page ❶

Before You Read

❶ Find a page with ...

1 a balloon   5 a house
2 a castle   6 red shoes
3 a dog   7 a witch
4 a forest

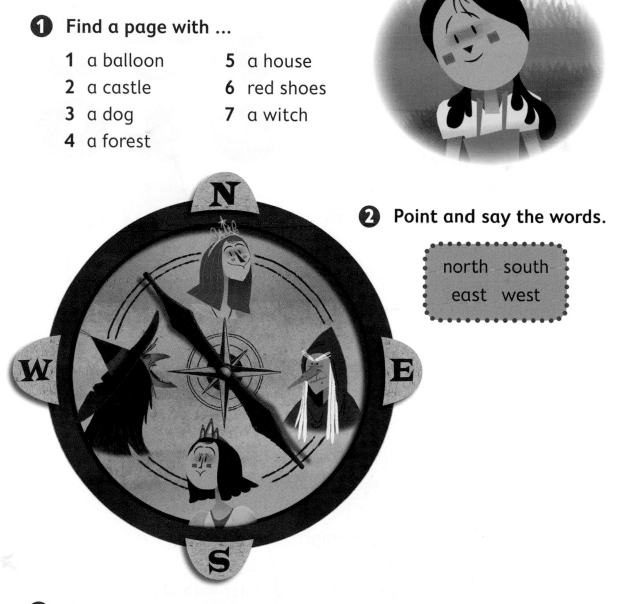

❷ Point and say the words.

north   south
east   west

❸ There are four witches and one wizard in this story. Do you know any other stories about witches and wizards?

Activity page ❷

After You Read

❶ Point and say the name.

> Dorothy Toto The Tin Man
> The Lion The Scarecrow
> the yellow brick road
> The Wizard of Oz
> The Bad Witch of the West
> The Good Witch of the North

❷ Where does it happen? Match.

1 Dorothy and Toto hide under the bed.
2 Dorothy helps the Tin Man.
3 Dorothy talks to the Wizard of Oz.
4 Dorothy washes the floors.
5 Dorothy clicks her shoes.

a the City of Oz
b the good witch's castle
c the house
d the forest
e the bad witch's castle

❸ Read and answer Yes (Y) or No (N).

1 Dorothy's house kills the Bad Witch of the East. ☐
2 The Scarecrow wants to be brave. ☐
3 The Tin Man wants to be smart. ☐
4 The Lion does not want to be a coward. ☐
5 Dorothy kills the Bad Witch of the West with water. ☐
6 The Wizard arrived in Oz in a balloon. ☐
7 Dorothy goes back home in the balloon. ☐